EDGE BOOKS™

COURAGE
UNDER FIRE

U.S. AIR FORCE TRUE STORIES

TALES OF BRAVERY

by Adam Miller

CAPSTONE PRESS
a capstone imprint

Edge Books are published by Capstone Press,
1710 Roe Crest Drive, North Mankato, Minnesota 56003
www.capstonepub.com

Library of Congress Cataloging-in-Publication Data
Miller, Adam, 1970–
U.S. Air Force true stories : tales of bravery / by Adam Miller.
    pages cm—(Edge books. Courage under fire)
Includes bibliographical references and index.
Summary: "Provides gripping accounts of Air Force servicemen and servicewomen who
showed exceptional courage during combat"—Provided by publisher.
Audience: Ages 8–12.
ISBN 978-1-4765-9936-6 (library binding)
ISBN 978-1-4765-9941-0 (eBook PDF)
1. United States. Air Force—Juvenile literature. 2. Airmen—United States—Juvenile
literature. 3. Courage—Juvenile literature. I. Title. II. Title: USAF true stories.
UG633.M368 2015
358.40092'273—dc23   2014004262

Editorial Credits
Christopher L. Harbo, editor; Veronica Scott, designer; Gene Bentdahl, production specialist

Photo Credits
Corbis, 7, Bettmann, 8; Getty Images: Popperfoto, 9, Time & Life Pictures/Dick Swanson,
18, Time & Life Pictures/Frank Scherschel, 12; iStockphotos: lauradyoung, 5 (SS); NARA,
13, 14; Newscom: Everett Collection, 6; Shutterstock: Jim Barber, 5 (DSC), R Carner, 5 (PH);
Smithsonian National Air and Space Museum (WEB10053-2004), 29; U.S. Air Force photo, 10,
11, 15, 16, 19, 20, 21, 27, 2nd Lt. Keavy Rake, 25, Capt. Justin T. Watson, 28, Senior Airman
Grovert Fuentes-Contreras, 23, Staff Sgt. Michael B. Keller, cover (inset), Staff Sgt. Ryan Crane,
cover, 3; Wikimedia: U.S. Air Force, 5 (AFDFC); Wikipedia: DoD photo, 5, 17, 18 (MOH), U.S.
Air Force, 5 (AFC)

Design Elements
Shutterstock: Filipchuk Oleg Vasiliovich, locote, Oleg Zabielin, Petr Vaclavek

Direct Quotations
Page 21 from "Operation Iraqi Freedom Hero Shares Her Story" by Stacie N. Shafran, U.S. Air
    Force (www.af.mil/News/ArticleDisplay/tabid/223/Article/117270/operation-iraqi-
    freedom-hero-shares-her-story.aspx).

Printed in the United States of America in Stevens Point, Wisconsin
032014   008092WZF14

TABLE OF CONTENTS

DAWN OF THE AIR FORCE

The Air Force is the U.S. military's youngest branch. It started in 1907 as the Aeronautical Division of the Army Signal Corps. This division took charge of military balloons and other air machines. Within one year the division tested its first airplane.

While the Aeronautical Division started small, wars soon brought rapid growth. Just before World War I (1914–1918), the division became the Aviation Section. Then in 1918 America's air forces were renamed the Air Service of the U.S. Army. During nine months of World War I, Air Service pilots shot down 756 enemy aircraft.

By World War II (1939–1945), the Air Service became the Air Corps. It included about 26,500 men and 2,200 aircraft. Then in 1942 the War Department changed the Air Corps into the Army Air Forces. By the end of World War II, more than 2 million men and women and 63,700 aircraft served this huge organization.

On September 18, 1947, the Army Air Forces changed names one last time. The U.S. Air Force finally became its own military branch. But through its long history, one thing has not changed. Its members have served bravely and have taken part in every U.S. war. Now you'll meet several of its men and women who showed exceptional courage under fire.

MILITARY AWARDS

Medal of Honor:
the highest award for bravery
in the U.S. military

Distinguished Service Cross:
the second-highest military award
for bravery that is given to members
of the U.S. Army (and Air Force
prior to 1960)

Air Force Cross:
the second-highest military award
for bravery that is given to members
of the Air Force

Silver Star:
the third-highest award for bravery
in the U.S. military

Purple Heart:
an award given to members of
the military wounded by the enemy
in combat

Distinguished Flying Cross:
an award given to members of the
military who show extraordinary
achievement in flight

WORLD WAR I

DATES: 1914–1918

THE COMBATANTS: ALLIES (MAIN COUNTRIES: GREAT BRITAIN, FRANCE, ITALY, RUSSIA, UNITED STATES) VS. CENTRAL POWERS (MAIN COUNTRIES: GERMANY, AUSTRIA-HUNGARY, BULGARIA, OTTOMAN EMPIRE)

THE VICTOR: ALLIES

CASUALTIES: ALLIES–5,142,631 DEAD; CENTRAL POWERS–3,386,200 DEAD

Lieutenant Frank Luke Jr. stands beside one of the German observation balloons he shot down on September 18, 1918.

SECOND LIEUTENANT FRANK LUKE JR.

The United States entered World War I in April 1917. Shortly after, Frank Luke Jr. joined the U.S. Army Signal Corps' Aviation Section. In July 1918 he went to France to fly in the 27th Aero **Squadron**.

Luke's squadron had orders to destroy German observation balloons. These balloons helped the Germans see the battlefields below and plan their ground attacks. Luke and his friend Lieutenant Joseph Frank Wehner worked together on these daredevil missions. Luke attacked the balloons while Wehner defended him from enemy planes. The two ducked and dodged their way around German fighter planes. During seven days in September, Luke shot down 13 enemy aircraft. Then on September 18, Wehner and Luke got caught in a **dogfight**. Wehner attacked the German fighter, allowing Luke to take out his target. But the fighter shot down Wehner, killing him.

squadron—a group of ships, soldiers, or other military units
dogfight—a mid-air battle between fighter planes

Losing his partner made Luke more determined on his missions than ever. Eleven days later he hunted down three more German balloons. He quickly shot down the first two. After taking out the last balloon, a German soldier fired from a distant hill. The bullet gravely wounded Luke, forcing him to land behind enemy lines. Drawing his gun, Luke took out several German soldiers before dying. For his courage Luke was **posthumously** awarded the Medal of Honor. The Luke Air Force Base in Arizona was also named after him.

Frank Luke Jr. with his airplane

posthumous—coming or happening after death

WORLD WAR II

DATES: 1939–1945

THE COMBATANTS: ALLIES (MAIN COUNTRIES: GREAT BRITAIN, FRANCE, RUSSIA, UNITED STATES) VS. AXIS POWERS (MAIN COUNTRIES: GERMANY, ITALY, JAPAN)

THE VICTOR: ALLIES

CASUALTIES: ALLIES—14,141,544 DEAD; AXIS—5,634,232 DEAD

An Air Force bomber pilot speaks to his crew during World War II.

SERGEANT JOHN FOLEY

John Foley joined the Army Air Forces in November 1941. Just one month later, the United States entered World War II after Japan attacked Pearl Harbor. Without even going through basic training, Foley shipped out to an airbase in Brisbane, Australia.

Foley's main job at the base was cleaning the bomber guns. One of those bombers was a B-26 flown by Lieutenant Walter Krell. When Krell's **turret** gunner got injured, he started looking for a replacement. Krell liked Foley's work on the guns so he asked if Foley could take the job.

Foley got a crash course on using the gun turret. With only a day and a half of training, he flew into combat. It turned out he was a natural with the weapon. Foley shot down a Japanese Zero fighter plane on his very first mission. Two weeks later he took down two more Zeros.

Sergeant John Foley (center, kneeling) with the other crew members of his B-26 bomber.

Foley (right) serving as an instructor at the AAF Gunnery School in Fort Myers, Florida.

A war reporter heard about Foley and nicknamed him "Johnny Zero." Soon the heroism of "Johnny Zero" caught people's attention back in the United States. A hit song called "Johnny Got a Zero" even made it onto the radio. Foley was famous. Meanwhile Foley kept fighting. He shot down at least seven more planes in 32 missions. He also survived three crashes, one of which he was the only survivor.

In 1943 Foley caught **malaria** and returned to the United States. After a brief time as a gunnery instructor, he shipped out to England to fight as a B-24 gunner. He completed 31 missions in just 60 days. Still eager to fight, Foley volunteered for a third tour. Just as he was preparing to go, the war ended.

turret—a rotating, armored structure that holds a weapon on top of a vehicle

malaria—a serious disease that people get from mosquito bites; malaria causes high fever, chills, and sometimes death

TECHNICAL SERGEANT ARIZONA HARRIS

On January 3, 1943, Arizona Harris controlled the top turret of a B-17 named the Sons of Fury. This bomber was among 84 others on a mission to destroy Japanese submarines off the western coast of France. On the way there, antiaircraft fire blasted the Sons of Fury and three other bombers.

Bullets ripped through the Sons of Fury. Two engines shut down and the nose of the aircraft was blown away. Seriously wounded, the pilot and navigator did everything they could to control the bomber. Meanwhile, Harris took aim at six German fighters trying to blow the Sons of Fury out of the sky.

a formation of B-17 bombers during World War II

About 40 miles (64 kilometers) off the French coast, the Sons of Fury belly-landed in the Bay of Biscay. As the bomber sank, Harris continued firing his gun until his turret finally slipped beneath the waves. For his bravery fighting to the very end, Harris was posthumously awarded the Distinguished Service Cross.

A B-17 bomber helps destroy an aircraft factory in northern Poland during World War II.

THE KOREAN WAR

Dates: 1950–1953

The Combatants: the United States, South Korea, and United Nations (UN) troops vs. North Korea and China

The Victor: No victor; the UN and North Korea signed a truce, but no permanent peace treaty was ever signed by North Korea and South Korea

Casualties: United States, UN, and South Korea—256,631 dead; Chinese and North Koreans—estimated 1,006,000 dead

A group of F-86E Sabre fighter jets patrols the skies above Korea in 1953.

CAPTAIN MANUEL FERNANDEZ

Captain Manuel Fernandez never passed up a chance to fly during the Korean War. Between September 1952 and August 1953, he flew 124 combat missions and took out at least 14 enemy fighters. But his actions on March 21, 1953, best display his rank as the third-best flying **ace** of the war.

While flying over North Korea, Fernandez spotted a formation of 30 enemy fighters. Although heavily outnumbered he went on the attack. During his approach he tried dropping his extra fuel tanks to increase his speed. But only one tank dropped, limiting how well his plane could fly. Rather than give up the chase, he pushed ahead and caught up to the last two enemy fighters.

Fernandez opened fire on the two fighters. He peppered one fighter's wing and body with bullets. As he prepared for another attack, the second fighter attacked him. Fernandez quickly circled around and locked onto his attacker. With several quick bursts of gunfire, he took out the second fighter, causing its pilot to eject.

Fernandez then hunted down the first fighter he had hit. As he closed to within 150 feet (46 meters), his gunfire sent the fighter spiraling to the ground. For his courage in Korea, Fernandez earned the Distinguished Service Cross and the Silver Star.

ace—top fighter pilot

THE VIETNAM WAR

DATES: 1959–1975

THE COMBATANTS: UNITED STATES, SOUTH VIETNAM, AND THEIR ALLIES VS. NORTH VIETNAM AND ITS ALLIES

THE VICTOR: NORTH VIETNAM

CASUALTIES: UNITED STATES–58,220 DEAD; SOUTH VIETNAM–ESTIMATED 200,000 TO 250,000 DEAD; NORTH VIETNAM–ESTIMATED 1.1 MILLION DEAD

An AC-47 gunship flies over South Vietnam during the Vietnam War.

AIRMAN 1ST CLASS JOHN LEVITOW

On February 24, 1969, John Levitow flew on an AC-47 gunship during a night mission over South Vietnam. He was part of a crew dropping flares into a combat zone. These flares helped ground troops locate enemy positions.

Suddenly an enemy **mortar** blasted a 2-foot (0.6-m) hole in the wing of the plane. More than 40 pieces of burning **shrapnel** tore through Levitow's back and legs. Although bleeding and in pain, he helped move another injured man away from the open cargo door. Then he noticed a smoking flare among spilled ammunition on the aircraft floor.

In an instant Levitow realized the live flare was about to ignite. He tried to grasp it with his hands, but couldn't get a grip. Finally he threw himself on top of the flare and hugged it to his body. Then he slid to the back of the plane and shoved it out the cargo door. As the flare spun away through the air, it flashed white-hot. Levitow's quick thinking had saved the aircraft and his crew. For his bravery, he received the Medal of Honor.

mortar—a short cannon that fires shells or rockets high in the air
shrapnel—pieces that have broken off something after an explosion

CAPTAIN LANCE SIJAN

On November 9, 1967, Captain Lance Sijan and Colonel John Armstrong flew a bombing run over Laos. As they released their payload, the bombs exploded early and engulfed their F-4C Phantom fighter-bomber in flames. Armstrong died instantly, but Sijan ejected from the fiery wreck.

Sijan's parachute dropped him in the jungle below. Although he had escaped the crash, Sijan still suffered serious injuries. His right hand and left leg were broken. He had a fractured skull and deep cuts on his body. On top of that, he had no food and very limited survival gear.

The next day a search and rescue team picked up Sijan's distress signal. Although they tried several times, heavy enemy fire made a rescue impossible. The rescue mission was called off. Sijan was considered missing in action (MIA).

F-4C Phantom fighter-bomber

A group of F-4C Phantom fighter-bombers drops its bombs over North Vietnam in 1966.

Despite his injuries, Sijan dragged himself 3 miles (4.8 km) through the dense jungle. He survived for 45 days before being captured. In his prison cell, two other American prisoners of war (POWs) tried to mend Sijan's injuries. But his body never had a chance to heal. He was beaten and tortured on a regular basis. Through it all, he never gave up military secrets. Even though he was weak and injured, Sijan's will to survive remained strong. He even talked to fellow prisoners about plans for escape. But he eventually caught **pneumonia** and died on January 22, 1968.

For his courage and will to survive, Sijan was posthumously awarded the Medal of Honor. The Air Force further honored Sijan by creating the Lance P. Sijan Award. It honors Air Force men and women who show exceptional leadership.

pneumonia—a serious disease that causes the lungs to become inflamed and filled with a thick fluid that makes breathing difficult

OPERATION ENDURING FREEDOM

Dates: 2001–present

The Combatants: Afghanistan government, the United States and its coalition forces vs. al-Qaida **TERRORIST** organization and the Taliban, an Islamic group that supports al-Qaida

The Victor: Conflict ongoing

Casualties: American and coalition forces (through December 6, 2012)–3,215 dead; Afghan civilians (reported from January 2007 to June 2012)–13,009 dead; Taliban and al-Qaida–number unknown

Senior Airman Mark Forester with a group of Afghan children

SENIOR AIRMAN MARK FORESTER

On September 29, 2010, Mark Forester joined a team of Army Special Forces soldiers and Afghan National Army soldiers. Their mission was to attack **insurgents** in Jangalak Village. As they entered the village, heavy gunfire erupted. In order to call in air support, Forester put himself in the line of fire. But his efforts paid off when two attack helicopters provided cover for the team to reach a safer position.

As the battle raged on, a bullet fatally injured one of the Army soldiers. Forester immediately led a small group into enemy fire to retrieve him. During the rescue a bullet ripped through Forester's chest. Though fatally wounded, he continued to fight until his last breath. In the end Forester's actions helped take out 12 insurgents. The remaining members of the team were able to capture a stockpile of weapons and ammunition. For his bravery and sacrifice, Forester was posthumously awarded the Silver Star.

rorist—a person who uses violence to kill, injure, or make people and ernments afraid

urgent—a person who rebels and fights against his or her country's ng government and those supporting it

In June 2011 Angela Blue deployed to Forward Operating Base Sweeny in Afghanistan. As an aeromedical technician, her job was to help treat and **evacuate** soldiers wounded in battle.

Only one month after arriving, Blue's base came under attack. Grenades, mortars, and heavy machine gun fire pounded the compound. Blue received a radio call to help with injuries on the Afghan National Army side of the base. When she got there, she helped wounded soldiers while the base was still under attack. As she worked she noticed one patient bleeding beneath the **tourniquet** on his leg. She immediately put a second tourniquet on the leg to stop the bleeding. Blue's quick thinking saved his life.

Toward the end of her tour, Blue and her team traveled with Afghan soldiers on a resupply mission. Suddenly one of the Afghan Humvees hit a bomb called an improvised explosive device (IED). Blue raced to the scene to help the injured. While her team treated the soldiers with less serious wounds, she helped the more seriously wounded driver. Because of her team's quick action, everyone in the Humvee survived.

evacuate—to leave a dangerous place and go somewhere safer
tourniquet—a tight wrapping designed to prevent a major loss of blood from a wound

Blue in Shinkai,
Afghanistan, in 2011

Just three hours later, the truck Blue was riding in triggered another IED. Seriously wounded, she was immediately evacuated for medical help. When she recovered, Blue received the Purple Heart for her injuries. She also received several other military awards for her bravery during combat.

STAFF SERGEANT BEN SEEKELL

On May 8, 2011, Ben Seekell and his military working dog, Charlie, joined a security mission. As they returned to Bagram Airfield, they stepped on a land mine. The ground exploded, sending Seekell and Charlie sailing through the air. Not aware that his leg was almost completely torn off, Seekell tried calling out to members of his team. He was especially worried about his canine partner. Charlie suffered several shrapnel wounds and cowered in terror from the noise.

Seekell faced a long, painful recovery. He had five surgeries, which included the **amputation** of his foot. He also struggled through about five hours of intense **physical therapy** every day. But Seekell was determined to work with Charlie again. Only eight months after losing his foot, he passed the Air Force fitness test. Seekell once again returned to active duty with Charlie at his side.

amputation—the removal of an arm or a leg
physical therapy—the treatment of diseased or injured muscles and joints with exercise, massage, and heat

Seekell receives a visit from his working dog, Charlie, four months after becoming injured in Afghanistan.

STAFF SERGEANT ROBERT GUTIERREZ JR.

On October 5, 2009, Robert Gutierrez Jr. was working with an Army Special Forces unit. Their task was to take out a Taliban target in a small village in Afghanistan's Herat province. As a combat controller, Gutierrez's job was to call in air support during the mission.

As the unit entered the village, they came under heavy fire. When a fellow soldier's rifle jammed, Gutierrez jumped into his place. He took a bullet to the chest that collapsed his lung. The searing pain made it nearly impossible for him to breathe.

The unit's medic plunged a 7-inch (18-centimeter) needle into Gutierrez's chest to blow his lung back up. Then Gutierrez called in an F-16 and a gunship to clear out the enemy fighters firing on them.

Because of Gutierrez's actions, no U.S. soldiers were killed during the battle. For his bravery and heroism, he earned the Air Force Cross.

Gutierrez in
Afghanistan

OPERATION IRAQI FREEDOM

DATES: 2003–2011

THE COMBATANTS: THE UNITED STATES AND COALITION FORCES VS. IRAQ, FIRST THE GOVERNMENT OF SADDAM HUSSEIN AND THEN INSURGENTS

THE VICTOR: THE UNITED STATES DEFEATED SADDAM HUSSEIN IN 2003 BUT THEN FACED STIFF FIGHTING FROM INSURGENTS UNTIL ITS WITHDRAWAL IN 2011

CASUALTIES: AMERICAN AND COALITION FORCES—4,804 DEAD; IRAQI SOLDIERS AND INSURGENTS—ESTIMATED MORE THAN 30,000 DEAD

An A-10 Thunderbolt II aircraft flies over Iraq in 2006.

CAPTAIN KIM CAMPBELL

On April 7, 2003, Captain Kim Campbell flew her A-10 Thunderbolt II over Baghdad, Iraq. She was providing air support to ground troops when a massive jolt rocked her aircraft. An enemy surface-to-air missile had hit the tail of her fighter. Campbell recalled, "There was no question ... I knew I had been hit by enemy fire." The jet rolled left and pointed toward the ground. It didn't respond to any of Campbell's control inputs.

Campbell quickly used the manual override to gain control of the aircraft. The jet leveled off and she managed to fly back to the airbase. But Campbell knew landing would be difficult. Gripping the controls and remembering her flight training, she landed the crippled aircraft perfectly. For her courage that day Campbell received the Distinguished Flying Cross.

Campbell's heavily damaged A-10 Thunderbolt II

For more than 100 years, millions of U.S. airmen have proudly defended their country. Time and again, they have risked their lives—never thinking twice about putting themselves in harm's way. Their tales show us more than just the strength of our fighting men and women. They display the incredible depth of human courage in the line of fire.

amputation (am-pyuh-TAY-shun)—the removal of an arm or a leg

dogfight (DAWG-fite)—a mid-air battle between fighter planes

evacuate (i-VA-kyuh-wayt)—to leave a dangerous place and go somewhere safer

insurgent (in-SUR-junt)—a person who rebels and fights against his or her country's ruling government and those supporting it

malaria (muh-LAIR-ee-ah)—a serious disease that people get from mosquito bites; malaria causes high fever, chills, and sometimes death

mortar (MOR-tur)—a short cannon that fires shells or rockets high in the air

physical therapy (FIZ-uh-kuhl THER-uh-pee)—the treatment of diseased or injured muscles and joints with exercise, massage, and heat

pneumonia (nuh-MOH-nyuh)—a serious disease that causes the lungs to become inflamed and filled with a thick fluid that makes breathing difficult

posthumous (POHST-huh-muhss)—coming or happening after death

shrapnel (SHRAP-nuhl)—pieces that have broken off something after an explosion

squadron (SKWAH-druhn)—a group of ships, soldiers, or other military units

terrorist (TER-ur-ist)—a person who uses violence to kill, injure, or make people and governments afraid

tourniquet (TUR-nuh-ket)—a tight wrapping designed to prevent a major loss of blood from a wound

turret (TUR-it)—a rotating, armored structure that holds a weapon on top of a vehicle

Bozzo, Linda. *U.S. Air Force.* Serving in the Military. Mankato, Minn.: Amicus High Interest, 2014.

Heinrichs, Ann. *Voices of World War I: Stories from the Trenches.* Voices of War. Mankato, Minn.: Capstone, 2011.

Linde, Barbara M. *Heroes of the U.S. Air Force.* Heroes of the U.S. Military. New York: Gareth Stevens Publishing, 2013.

Williams, Brian. *Pilots in Peril.* War Stories. Chicago: Heinemann Library, 2012.

Arroyo, Rachel. "Combat Controller Posthumously Awarded Silver Star." Air Force Special Operations Command, June 15, 2012, www.afsoc.af.mil/news/story.asp?id=123306176.

Correll, John T. "The Legend of Frank Luke," Air Force Magazine, Vol. 92, No.8, August 2009, www.airforcemag.com/MagazineArchive/Pages/2009/August%202009/0809luke.aspx.

Frisbee, John L. "Valor: Unsung Heroes of World War II," Vol 76, No. 7, July 1993, www.airforcemag.com/MagazineArchive/Pages/1993/July%201993/0793valor.aspx.

Katzaman, Jim. "To Stem the Tide: A Korean War Perspective," U.S. Air Force. August 7, 2007, www.af.mil/News/ArticleDisplay/tabid/223/Article/126076/to-stem-the-tide-a-korean-war-perspective.aspx.

Laster, Jill. "Air Force Senior Airman Mark A. Forester." Military Times, http://projects.militarytimes.com/valor/air-force-senior-airman-mark-a-forester/4819219.

Patrick, Bethanne Kelly. "Capt. Lance Peter Sijan." Military.com, www.military.com/Content/MoreContent?file=ML_sijan_bkp.

Shafran, Stacie N. "Operation Iraqi Freedom Hero Shares Her Story," U.S. Air Force, March 18, 2010, www.af.mil/News/ArticleDisplay/tabid/223/Article/117270/operation-iraqi-freedom-hero-shares-her-story.aspx.

FactHound offers a safe, fun way to find Internet sites related to this book. All of the sites on FactHound have been researched by our staff.

Here's all you do:

Visit *www.facthound.com*

Type in this code: 9781476599366

Super-cool stuff! Check out projects, games and lots more at **www.capstonekids.com**